Doing Time with the Arts
The Koestler Trust at 50

Edited by Ariane Bankes

First published by the Koestler Trust 2012 to coincide with its annual exhibition

Free: Art by offenders, secure patients and detainees

Curated by Sarah Lucas

Royal Festival Hall, Southbank Centre, London

20 September – 25 November 2012

Koestler Trust
168a Du Cane Road
London
W12 0TX

Designed by Fagan Jones Communications Ltd
Printed by HM Prison Maidstone

A CIP catalogue record for this book is available from the British Library

ISBN: 978-0-9574101-0-7

Front Cover:
50, HM Prison Send, Bronze Award for Theme: '50' 2012
Back Cover:
Birthday cake decorated by Grayson Perry for the Koestler Trust's 50th anniversary
fundraising dinner

Contents

The Papacy, HM Prison Peterborough, Jeffrey Archer Platinum Award for Matchstick & Mixed Media Models 2012

THE PAPACY

How it All Began...

"Arthur Koestler's experiences [of political imprisonment in the Spanish Civil War and of campaigning against the death sentence in Britain] gave him the idea of establishing an annual prize (or prizes) for the best artistic work produced by prisoners who were still incarcerated. He was willing to set aside £400 a year from his royalties for the purpose, in the hope that others would support the venture as time went on...

'Being in prison leaves its imprint on you for the rest of your life', he had written earlier. 'This trauma can turn you into a neurotic, but it can also act as a stimulant with positive effects. The prisoner's worst enemy is boredom, depression, the slow death of thought.' Koestler's goal was to make the prisoner's life more bearable, to help him acquire something that would aid him in making a new start when he left the prison behind, and perhaps to 'discover the hidden talents within himself'....

David Astor [editor of the Observer and friend of Koestler] gave a lunch at the Waldorf-Astoria Hotel in Aldwych to form a steering committee. Despite his protests, Koestler's name was considered indispensable by the others to attract money and attention, and the Koestler Awards, as they were called, came into existence in 1962."

from Koestler: *The Indispensable Intellectual* by Michael Scammell (Faber, 2009)

On the Landing, HM Prison Whatton, Highly Commended Award for Craft 2012

'The painting *Despair* is obviously a self-portrait. It is beautifully painted, and so expressive it almost hurts to look at it. But the skill and painterliness overcomes the pain of the sitter/painter. We own many pictures by established artists as well as other Koestler contributors. This is among the most moving.'

Roger Graef, criminologist, film-maker and advisor to the Koestler Trust

On reading Swineherd
After: Eiléan Ni Chuilleanáin

When all this is over, said number 732
I will be open like a poem, read forward
Wide eyed, collecting smooth
Pebbles to sit in clay bowls. I will whisper to my terrier, share her
Delight at hidden snuffly paths. I mean to
Choose fruit carefully, haggle with a Welsh
Speaking butcher and bake my own bread.

When names are called I will walk on
When stones are thrown I can dance
Knocking on walls with happy taps.

As smiling troubadours strum sad tunes, and
Clowns daub glee lines on lips pointing south
I intend to stroll by, open like a poem.

The Derelict Detective, HM Prison Shepton Mallet, Highly Commended Award for Digital Image 2012. This piece was produced by the recipient of the 2011 William Arthur Rudd Scholarship and the 2012 Evelyn Plesch Scholarship.

DOING TIME WITH KOESTLER

James Crosbie

The first I heard of the Koestler Awards Scheme was when I was serving a sentence of three years 'corrective training' in Wandsworth Prison - which sentence, as it happens, failed to make the least impression on me. My introduction to 'The Koestler' came about when one afternoon I went back to my cell after a day's work chopping up stinking railway sleepers and found a pencil, two pages of lined A4 paper, an entry form and an information sheet inviting me to enter some sort of writing competition. I read the information sheet which explained that the A4 pages were for the purpose of submitting an entry for a competition that had been initiated by some guy called Arthur Koestler.

If I remember correctly there was a short explanation as to who this Arthur Koestler was and why he had sought the permission of the then Home Secretary, Rab Butler, to introduce, for the first time, a competition for the inmates of Her Majesty's Prisons. Apparently this Arthur Koestler, a well-known intellectual, writer and respected journalist, had gone over to Spain in 1936 during the Spanish Civil War to side with the Republicans against General Franco's Nationalist government. During the course of his activities there he had been captured and incarcerated in a Spanish jail as a prisoner of war and, indeed, even faced the death penalty. However, supporters of Koestler such as the Hearst newspaper group and the British Government intervened on his behalf and he was released on a prisoner exchange basis six months later and promptly left Spain for France.

Many years later, having settled in London, Koestler found himself thinking about his experience as prisoner in the Spanish jail. What he especially remembered was the complete lack of mental stimulation and the total boredom of being locked up in a prison cell with absolutely nothing to do and nothing to aim for. This was 'doing time' the hard way, and he realised that prisoners in Britain were in a similar situation to the one that he had found himself in when imprisoned in Spain. With the memory of his own experience strong in his mind, Koestler wondered if there was anything he could do to alleviate the boredom of incarceration. After a lot of thought he decided that he would try to organise and initiate some sort of competition that would interest the prisoners, both stimulating their minds and giving them something to do and a target to aim for.

Being a writer himself, his first thoughts leaned towards a writing competition with cash awards for success, which would give prisoners an incentive to enter. Giving the matter further thought, however, Koestler decided that if the competition was limited to writers alone it would deter the less literate from entering. Keen to get as many prisoners as possible involved, he decided to broaden the range of the competition to include music composition and painting, realising that painting especially would attract a wider range of entrant. Satisfied with his plans, Arthur finally presented his idea to the Home Secretary of the time, Rab Butler, who enthusiastically endorsed the plan and gave permission for the Koestler Awards Scheme to be initiated. This was the reason I found a pencil, an entry form and two sheets of lined A4 paper on my cell table that day.

Now would be a great time to say that I entered the competition and won an award, but unfortunately that was not the case - well, not on that occasion anyway. I vaguely remember writing a short essay on the benefits of travelling abroad and how it broadened the mind and all that. But at that stage in my life, never having left our shores, I was flogging a dead horse. I handed my effort in at the hall desk and that was the last I heard of it. However, although I didn't realise it at the time, unluckily for me I was going to have plenty of opportunities to enter the Koestler Awards again.

When I left the prison system after an abortive period (from society's point of view, that is) of so-called 'corrective training' I had learned how to rip open safes, hot-wire cars and, courtesy of a City and Guilds course in printing in Maidstone prison, forge all sorts of useful documents such as driving licences, insurance certificates and other forms and papers helpful to a criminal lifestyle.

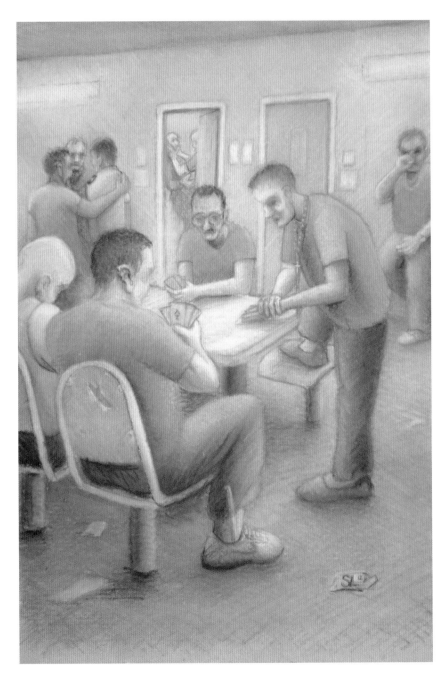

My next venture into the competitive world of the Koestler Awards took place many years later when, once again, the forces of law and order prevailed against me and, unfortunately, I found myself eligible to enter the competition again.

Needless to say the requirement for entry was that you had to be a guest in one of Her Majesty's concrete and steel-barred residencies reserved for the severely anti-social. Unfortunately I qualified in spades for this as I had, over several years, withdrawn huge amounts of money from the banking system (today I would be a hero!) without the benefit of having an account, thus avoiding the bothersome business of filling in withdrawal slips. In simple English, I had robbed them. For these misdemeanours and thanks to sterling work by the Glasgow Police Force I was given a 20-year special reservation in HMP Peterhead as one of Her Majesty's 'A' category guests. However, to paraphrase a little, 'As one door slams another door opens', and I found myself once again eligible to enter the competitive world of the Arthur Koestler Awards. Hurrah!

Like Arthur Koestler, I found that the hardest part of my sentence was the enforced idleness, the misery of having nothing to do. Certainly there were work parties during the day, but after work, once behind the door, boredom reigned. There was very little to occupy the mind, certainly nothing interesting or stimulating, and boredom can be very frustrating. Then a notice appeared inviting inmates to enter the annual Koestler Awards Scheme. I recalled my first attempt in 1962, and although interested I did not think I stood much of a chance and did not offer an entry. However, the following year, inspired by the success of another prisoner who had actually won an award, I decided to submit an entry myself.

I can only remember the name of the guy who won that award as John, but I knew him quite well and when word came through that he had been awarded first prize in the playwriting category it gave all the cons in Peterhead a lift. His success was noted by the Scottish press and announced on the local radio station. There was a collective feeling of pride among the other prisoners at John's success because, here at last, we had a guy in Peterhead prison getting good positive publicity. John had shown the public that we weren't all just a pack of low-life, uneducated criminals and everyone was very impressed. I congratulated John on his success and he gave me a copy of his play to read. His work impressed me too, and I immediately made up my mind to enter the following year's competition myself.

I had read John's play and felt I could reach at least the same standard of work. My interest and enthusiasm led me to enrol in English classes and from being bored, uninterested and apathetic I became suddenly stimulated and interested in things again. From then on my life in prison took on a more positive aspect. I found myself engrossed in researching and writing my book and play and suddenly life in prison became much more bearable.

Having amassed a large fund of exciting memories I had no difficulty in penning a crime novel, *Pay Day for Some*, as well as a short play about crooked police, *Public Service*, both of which I entered into the relevant categories of the Koestler competition.

It seemed a long wait but after several months I was delighted to be told that I had won First Prize with the novel and joint First Prize with the play. Being temporarily the blue-eyed boy of the Governor now, I lost no time in putting in a request that I be allowed to use my prize money to purchase a portable typewriter so as to further my literary ambitions and try to become an honest citizen through the medium of writing. Well, owing to my Koestler success, they could hardly refuse me and so I became the first prisoner, certainly in the Scottish prison system, to be allowed a typewriter in his cell. For that I gratefully thank and acknowledge Arthur Koestler for giving me the opportunity to obtain this privilege.

The sense of achievement I got from winning gave me immense satisfaction and spurred my determination to continue with my writing so I could enter the following year's competition. The most important thing, however, was that taking part in the Koestler Awards Scheme dramatically altered my attitude to doing time in prison. It made me realise that instead of mentally vegetating in my cell, I could work on something constructive that would exercise and stimulate my mind, keep me occupied and kill time, exactly as Arthur Koestler had intended. The Koestler Awards gave me something worthwhile to do and an objective to aim for. It was a challenge that banished the boredom of being behind the door; the very essence of Koestler's original plan. Time has proved his idea to be more than successful.

Since the Scheme's small beginnings in 1962, with just three original categories, the range has grown enormously. Matchstick modelling, marquetry and calligraphy are just three examples of subjects added to the original list; the writing categories alone have expanded to include short stories and novels, poetry, stage plays, TV and radio plays and screenwriting as well as journalism. The art category, too, has grown to include most types of painting and drawing art forms. And room has also been found to include fashion design, hair styling and beauty treatments that attract female entrants. Such a wide and inclusive range encourages most inmates to take part in some area of the competition, and the Koestler Trust has gone from strength to strength with more than 8,000 entries in

2012, its 50th anniversary year. Arthur Koestler's original vision has certainly borne fruit, as the ever growing popularity of the competition continues to bear witness.

There is no question that the challenge of the Koestler Awards and the feeling of achievement when my entries won had a far greater rehabilitative effect on me than any rehabilitation programme offered by the prison system. So much so that when I was finally released I was inspired to continue with my writing ambitions and was eventually successful in having my autobiography, *It's Criminal*, published. It was first published in hardback and was later reissued as a paperback under the title *Armed and Dangerous*. This caused several readers to write to me and complain that they had enjoyed reading *It's Criminal* so much that they had rushed out to buy *Armed and Dangerous*, only to find that it was the same book! 'Yes,' I diligently wrote back to each of them, 'but you must remember that *It's Criminal* after all.' Nobody replied to that one, but I like to think that I gave my correspondents something to laugh about and tell their mates.

Since leaving prison and joining the straight and narrow I have found life to be a lot more interesting than constantly being involved in the activities of my previous lifestyle. I meet a very different class of person now and life has become considerably more tranquil and satisfying, too. I am always busy, either writing articles or editing manuscripts for other aspiring writers. Currently, I have another novel about to be published and one more to follow soon after that. I must admit, however, that I rely quite heavily on my previous life for story-lines. I suppose what I am writing now could be described as faction, retro-crime novels which are a mixture of fact and fiction, you might say. It is, after all, the subject I am most qualified in.

There is no doubt that I have the Koestler Trust to thank for inspiring me to make greater efforts with my writing which resulted in my becoming a 'published' author. And it is a fact that doing time with Koestler made life that much more bearable than simply being locked away and forgotten in a concrete box. The Koestler Awards kept me interested and occupied throughout my time in prison and continues to do so beyond the confinement of a locked cell. I find it almost amusing now that from having my initial entry away back in 1962 apparently dismissed, I am now one of the judges in the Short Story writing category. Another interesting fact is that my fellow judge in last year's competition was a retired professor of English at St Andrews University, while I was a secondary school reject without a certificate to my name. Yet, out of forty or so entries, without any cross-reference or consultation with one another, we both chose the same Gold, Silver and Bronze awards. I have to admit I took great satisfaction from that and I have a lot to thank Arthur Koestler for. Indeed, doing time with Koestler has quite literally changed my life.

A Tale of Three Cities, HM Prison Inverness, The Co-operative Gold Award for Oil or Acrylic 2010

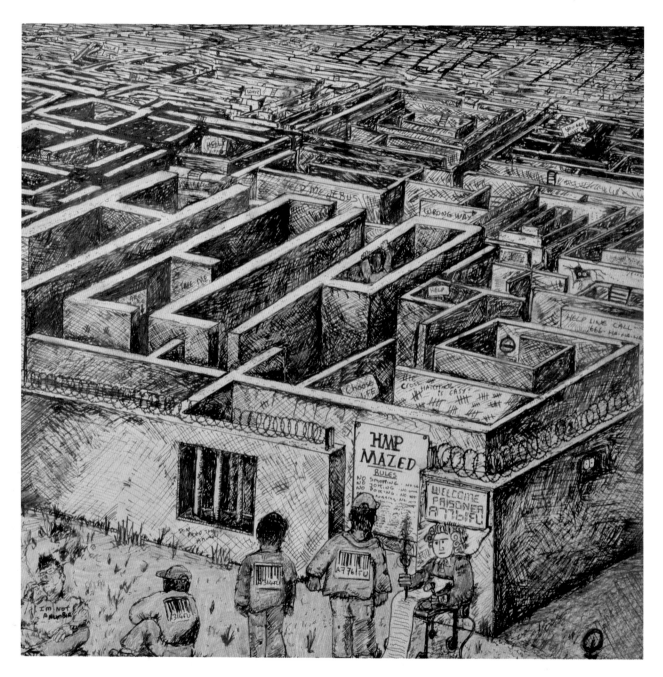

'I enjoyed this picture because it seemed to me to capture the bleak bewilderment which overcomes so many prisoners. Of course there are some very bad people in prison. But most of the men I've met inside are cases of 'there but for fortune go you or me.' I do not seek to excuse crime - and nor, frankly, do most of the prisoners I've met. But we'd all do well to consider how we'd fare if life seemed like this.'

Jeremy Paxman, broadcaster who judged the themed category 'Help!' for the 2011 Koestler Awards

Cubist Quilt, HM Prison Wandsworth, Norman Franklin Highly Commended Award for Needlecraft 2011

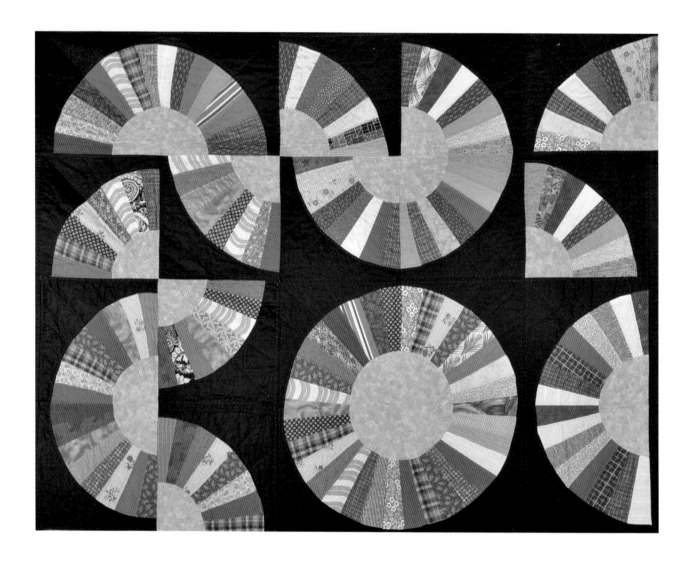

Telephone, HM Prison Pentonville, Bowen Smart Highly Commended Award for Matchstick &
Mixed Media Models 2012

'I really liked these two. The more I looked at them, the more they amused me and the fonder I grew of them. I enjoyed the confidence and vigour of the piece, and the affection with which these two great characters were depicted. We were unanimous that this artwork deserved the platinum prize.'

Lucy Astor, daughter of David Astor who helped Arthur Koestler to found the Koestler Awards in 1962

'Fifty – What Does it Mean to you?'

Voice 1: Let's talk about fifty, people, what does it mean to you?

Voice 2: 50? Isn't he an American rapper? Give me 2pac or Biggy anyway.

Voice 3: I think fifty sheep or calves would make a herd. Not a very big herd but a herd nonetheless. Is that enough?

Voice 4: 50 metres of woollen carpet is not cheap. Even in the sales you'll pay £10 per square metre. What a rip-off! - choose small houses with small rooms to avoid the carpet trap.

Voice 5: I was sitting on the No. 50 bus to Norbury with my little sister when a group of boys ran upstairs and started shouting and screaming at us, demanding money. They slashed me with a razorblade, just underneath my left eye. When I said I didn't have any, my sister peed herself and spent 3 hours in Mayday A&E in a wet skirt, waiting for the cut to be stitched. It was a bad night. Now I try to avoid using the 50 bus.

Voice 6: It's nothing - a number. I like 22, it's symbolic. Religion like 3, 7 and 9. There must be something in it. 50p buys you half a nine at Poundland. They'd go crazy if you tried it, though.

Voice 7: I've got fifty days to go. I can't wait to get a fresh start. Won't be long and I'll be on the other side of the gates.

Voice 8: My Grandfather lived at Number 50. The house had a shiny black door and stained glass panels. A long strip of fly-catching paper was pinned to the hall ceiling. It was always black with flies.

Voice 9: You can't and you shouldn't eat fifty of anything. It's too much. Even cherries.

Voice 10: The over 50s are the fastest growing group in the prison population of the United Kingdom.

Voice 11: 50 is the new 30!

Voice 12: Nah, 50's not the new 30! The only person who would say that is a woman over 40 who's worried about getting old. Let's be real here: no girl would ever say that, would they. Teenagers think 50 is old. And come to think of it, so do I.

Voice 13: Can you imagine having size 50 feet? Now those would be big feet. And I mean big. You'd have to order everything custom-made. That would be expensive. And if you had a 50-inch waist to match, then you'd have to go around naked and shoeless.

Voice 14: If you only have 50 friends on Facebook, you are a loser. Fifty is pathetic. Me? I don't use Facebook at all.

Voice 15: Very few people live to 50 where I'm from in Sierra Leone. We die in our 30s, even if we survive infancy.

Voice 16: The vet told me my dog Shiva had a 50/50 chance of pulling through. Stupidly, I thought they were good odds at the time. I thought she'd make it. She died on the morning of the 3rd December. You can keep your 50/50.

Voice 17: Fifty is an important milestone in companies since it marks the point where an organisation becomes an institution. You've made it, Koestler Trust. You will survive and prosper. You are now part of the establishment.

Voice 18: When I was 50, I wanted to retire and emigrate to

Bulgaria. I've changed my mind now, and I just wanna live in Soho.

Voice 19: I used to get ten shillings, which is today's 50 pence, for my pocket money every week. It went a hell of a long way. I could visit the sweet shop on the way to and back from school every day, and have a bit left over to spend at Woolworth's at the weekend. I can still taste those orange frozen jubblies, sherbet fountains and flying saucers.

Voice 20: People who follow Kabbalah believe there are 50 impurities. But I don't know what they are.

Voice 21: 50? I won't even see 50. I make my living on road hustling and three friends of mine have been killed in South London since Christmas this year. That's what goes down on the roads. It's too late for me. But I don't want my son to get involved with gangs. Maybe then he will reach 50.

Voice 22: This is the voice of HMP Brixton, and those were our reflections on the number 50.

Pink Wabbit, Peaks Unit, Rampton Hospital, Recycling or Papier Mache Category 2012

'During the selection there were mixed feelings about the pink rabbit, not on my part. Can a pink rabbit arouse controversy?'

Sarah Lucas, artist and curator of the 2012 Koestler Trust exhibition at Southbank Centre

HM Prison Swinfen Hall's contribution to the one-off art book *Koestler Trust: 50 artworks for 50 years,* which was auctioned at the Trust's 50th anniversary dinner

'The urge to escape understandably provides a common inspiration for art made in prisons: hence the prevalence of dream landscapes, depictions of a lost home or an imagined love object. But this powerful image refuses any easy or comforting fantasy: in black and white, it literally grapples in with the brute fact of imprisonment, making it clear that the bars and chains are as much inside the prisoner's head as outside it, constraining expression and denying identity.'

Rupert Christiansen, arts journalist and Koestler supporter

IRONY

The Rioter

So, we're the only black boys in this place?
I would have stayed down South: there was no space.
A Londoner? Same here! When you get in?
A month ago? You missed the rioting!
It's just as well: you'd be here all the same,
Just with a longer sentence to your name.
The feds[a] are on the hunt for everyone
And judges are just slamming man[b] for fun.
Girls too: all named in papers, to disgrace.
You check the news? You might have seen my case!

The Non-Rioter

I saw the news of riots on Sunday.
I called the fam[c] to check they were OK.
Later that day I saw the same again,
With other ends[d] in London jumping in.
Man hooded up as far as I could see,
Helping themselves like everything was free!
I don't know why the cops were holding back.

I think that they were just too scared to act.
North, South, East, West all got it, I would say -
But not Central: man seemed to stay away.

The West Midlands got onto the unrest:
Licked[e] bare shops, even licked shots[e] at the feds.
When those man got killed out in Birmingham,
I started hearing 'bout a next attack:
An Asian plan to start a massacre;
Muslims, Hindus and Sikhs against the blacks.
In London I saw so called 'EDL'.
Bare racial tension out there, I could tell.
It seemed to me like blacks against the rest;
Armed Turks in North and Sikhs with swords in West.

Some cities took a while to start their thing,
Like Mancs, but once they started, they went in.
And some did minor things that made no gwop[f]
They didn't even seem to target cops.
They acted up to make themselves look 'hard',
To say 'We did it, just like all the rest',
So when we look back on England in flames,
They can stand up and say they played their part.
'Cause if when England burns you won't join in,

How can you say your ends is on this ting^g?
You did what I'd have done if I were free:
Take everything, chase feds and run the streets.
'Cause even though the cities burned like hell,
With mob rule: vandalism, arson, theft,
It all looked so surreal and made me feel
Like it was the worst time to be in jail.
I could have been there, eating for myself
Instead of watching news, but that was cool:
Identifying vicariously,
The people out there rioting were me.

The Rioter

It's better you were locked up than were free:
You saw more of the rioting than me!
And now I'll be locked up 'til God knows when.
Regrettable? I'd do it all again!
The one lesson I'm wise enough to take:
I lack wisdom to learn from my mistakes.
But you should learn to never glory in
A waste of lives, of cities, houses, shops.
It's funny, you said 'Everything was free!'
I'm not free: I'm locked up! The irony.

'"Irony" shows a keen awareness of plotting and timing, as well as an admirable control of traditional form. The language is vivid and credible. Emotion is both conveyed and considered in perspective; I think we may hear more from this writer in a wider world, and I wish him very well.'

Lachlan Mackinnon, poet and Koestler Awards judge

[a]Feds: police
[b]Man: colloquial plural of man
[c]Fam: family (and close friends)
[d]Ends: local area, parts of a town or city
[e]Lick: raid, steal. Lick shots: to shoot (a gun)
[f]Gwop: money
[g]On this ting: seriously engaged in criminality

'This pencil drawing is charged with longing for the absent couple depicted, but also resonates a pride and direct connection between the subject and the artist which is a strong private conversation in itself. We are privileged to look in from outside at this letter home and are rewarded with a very sophisticated graphic arrangement reminiscent of Hockney in it's 'marriage of styles'. *I Love You Grandad* is a very moving and interesting drawing and it is hard enough to achieve either one of those things let alone both.'

Alan Kane, artist and Koestler Awards judge

WHAT GOOD ARE THE ARTS IN PRISON?

John Carey

Most people who are interested in the role that art can play in prisons are, I suppose, primarily concerned with prisoners and what can be done to help them. With me it was the other way round. I started by being primarily concerned with art. About ten years ago my editor at Faber and Faber, Julian Loose, said to me at lunch one day, 'Why don't you write a book about whether the arts do any good - whether they make people better?' The question didn't come out of the blue. Julian had noticed, in things I had written previously, my scepticism about claims that artistic people are morally and spiritually superior to the rest of humanity. Now he wanted me to give it serious thought, book-length.

Once I started, several problems became apparent. What does making people better mean? How can you tell that they have been made better? If they have been made better, how can you tell art was responsible? Over the next year or so I read everything I could get hold of that touched on these issues. I found that, on the first question, there was fairly general agreement that people become better by becoming more unselfish. However, there seems to be no evidence that people's encounters with works of arts have this effect on them - or, indeed, any moral effect at all. In their monumental study *Psychology of the Arts,* based on over a hundred years of findings in experimental psychology, Hans and Shulamith Kreitler conclude that works of art cannot be expected to produce behavioural changes in their recipients. Behaviour is a product of many and varied conditions of nature and nurture which cannot be created or modified by works of art.

My book, published in 2005 under the title *What Good Are the Arts?*, incorporated findings of this sort, and was greeted by art lovers with shrieks of rage. In the acrimonious reviews and angry debates that followed there was, however, a notable lack of any actual evidence that overturned - or, indeed, made the slightest dent in - the book's conclusions. In looking for that kind of evidence myself, the one area I found encouraging was art in prisons – or, rather, the reports of those engaged in it. A useful book was *Including the Arts: The Route to Basic and Key Skills in Prisons,* published in 2001 and still available on the Internet. Its central statement is made by the documentary film-maker and criminologist Roger Graef, who believes that art, as well as crime, is ultimately an expression of violence, and that, seen in the prison-context, an essential difference between them is that art can accommodate prisoners' violent feelings in a way that enhances their lives instead of damaging them. Experience of working in prisons has shown him that taking part in the making of art 'dramatically improves inmates' attitudes and behaviour'. Performance in operas, musicals and dramas 'gives voice to the anguish, pain and confusion that each inmate felt was only their private hell'.

What impressed me about Graef's testimony was that it was based on observing the effects of participation in the actual making of art, as opposed to the passive 'appreciation' or 'reception' of works of art which is what 'art education' often aims to teach, and which the Kreitlers' conclusions related to. The

chapter on drama-based arts in prison by Pauline Gladstone and Angus McLewin drove home this point. It reported on a wide range of drama companies that worked in prisons, and in each case the aim was to engage prisoners in the action, not treat them as spectators. Geese Theatre, for example, ran a course of plays and workshops with violent offenders, allowing them to act out violence and examine the cognitive processes behind it. Post-course evaluation showed a 20% reduction in the propensity to violent or hostile feelings and expressions. In 1999, prisoners at HMP Bullingdon, with help from The Irene Taylor Trust, put on a musical version of *Julius Caesar.* The Prison Adjudication Sheets of those who took part showed a 58% reduction in offending behaviour from six months before to six months following the project.

Witnesses of prison drama productions are left in no doubt that ideas about art as a lightning-conductor for violence have real substance. Libby Purves, attending an adapted *Macbeth* put on in HMP Pentonville by London Shakespeare Workout, writes:

It made your hair stand on end from the first moment when a dozen men flung themselves on the floor and crawled hissing like Gollum around our feet... This circle of men play the emotion of the piece: they are the witches and clowns, but also the temptation, the spirits of cruelty conjured by Lady Macbeth, the physical symbols of compulsion, remorse and mocking, snarling violence in the human heart which - as any prisoner knows - can turn either outwards or inwards.

Talking to the actors afterwards, Purves finds that they are alive to the power of whatever it is that has taken them over - 'It's very intense, very. It carries you' - and want to do something like it themselves: 'I'm going to try and write something. It's opened up my head'. Lives are changed. LSW keeps in touch with prisoners after their release. Ex-offenders come back and take part in productions, including the one Purves watched.

Besides providing a means of mastering violence, the arts in prison build self-confidence and self-esteem. All the contributors to *Including the Arts* stress this. Routine prison education-classes often do the opposite, confronting prisoners with their disabilities. But the arts are different. As Gladstone and McLewin put it, they 'start from where people are'. They are accessible to almost everyone. They give many prisoners their first experience of a positive and absorbing activity and, through contact with an arts educator, their first link with someone who is interested in what they can do rather than what they cannot. The confidence gained can, in turn, improve performance in numeracy and literacy classes.

The success of art in prison may not, it is true, be solely attributable to art. Simply to be treated as a human being and to co-operate on friendly terms with cultured, educated people, could be a transforming experience for prisoners if they were being taught first-aid or fly-fishing rather than art. Clive Hopwood, in his chapter on the Writers in Residence in Prisons scheme, recognises that getting the undivided attention of a real live professional writer for a 30-minute session is itself a boost to the self-valuation of someone who has been told all his life that he is a failure and has let his loved ones down. However, art seems to give prisoners something

else as well, and Graef's point about art as the expression of violence points to a psychological gain that goes beyond social acceptance.

A more serious issue is the difficulty prisoners have in keeping their interest in art alive after their release. Peter Cameron, an ex-offender who took a Koestler Trust course in prison, and is now a professional artist, testifies to this.

> It is important to grasp the fact that it is easier to take up arts activities inside than it is outside. Art is something that would bypass most people in their normal lives. I have spoken to many inmates and former inmates who have said exactly this – they never knew they liked or valued art – it had never been on the menu.

It is not only the difficulty of getting hold of materials that turns people off art after leaving prison. The arts feel accessible in prison because of personal contact with writers and artists. But on release ex-offenders find the art world 'elitist', and its 'posh buildings' intimidating. The result is predictable. Research shows that while prisoners engage actively in the arts on the inside, this is rarely continued beyond prison.

This is the situation that the Koestler Trust Arts Mentoring is designed to remedy. A 3-year pilot scheme, set up in 2007, trained professional artists, writers and musicians as Arts mentors and matched them with 50 offenders for one year after their release. The University of London independently evaluated the pilot scheme to assess its effectiveness, and as a result the Paul Hamlyn Foundation has agreed to continue funding the project.

The reports of mentors and mentees indicate that the scheme addresses precisely that sense of loss and abandonment that offenders had previously experienced on release. A typical case is that of John, who was sentenced to 5 years in prison for robbery in 2007, and whose interest in art was first picked up by a prison visitor. A prison art tutor recommended that he should apply to the Koestler mentoring scheme, and in June 2011 he completed his year-long course of 10 sessions with his mentor Johanna. Now he is studying Fine Art at Central St Martin's School of Art and Design. When he looks back on the progress he has made since his release, it was his personal one-to-one relationship with his mentor and his sense of her knowledge, authority and friendship that mattered above everything else. As he wrote at the time:

> Johanna knows a vast amount about art. We have been to galleries together, and not only has she supported me, she has helped me understand things that tutors and other people might not. She has been a huge help. I look forward to my mentoring meetings so much – it's so nice to have someone that is just there for me and my art, she's my lifeline.

If I were writing my book now, instead of way back in 2005, the Koestler Mentoring Scheme would provide its culmination, and I would use it as an example of how things ought to be managed in a civilized society. I should argue that a large proportion of whatever public money is available for the arts should be directed towards this scheme – and similar schemes that might grow out of it – and that these schemes should take precedence over the flagship enterprises such as the Royal Opera House Covent Garden which currently receive such colossal allocations of public funds. This reallocation of resources would, I'd suggest, help to mend our broken society, whereas the flagship enterprises, which intensify the impression that the arts are the preserve of the wealthy, increase its brokenness.

I can well see that these proposals might not meet with universal acclaim. However, discussion of them would bring into the open how serious we are – or are not – about redeeming and reclaiming the lives of the members of our society whom at present we simply lock up.

Solitary, HM Prison Lowdham Grange, Silver Award for Portraits 2012

Colnbrook Immigration Removal Centre's contribution to the one-off art book *Koestler Trust: 50 artworks for 50 years,* which was auctioned at the Trust's 50th anniversary dinner

'This moving sketch captures the bewilderment and heartbreak of immigration, and confers the dignity of public record on a humiliating and stressful personal experience. It reminds me of how I must have felt when I arrived in England as a child more than sixty years ago, clinging on to my mother and staring fearfully at this strange land which eventually became my home.'

Marina Lewycka, novelist and Koestler Trust supporter

'This portrait is from a series, it's obviously from life, there is a living person in front of the artist, and that psychological relationship is tangible, if not heightened even, as we know it is painted in a prison. I liked it so much that I bought it.'

Jeremy Deller, artist and winner of the Turner Prize in 2004, who judges the Portraits category for the Koestler Trust

FREEDOM OF EXPRESSION

A dialogue between William Muir and Graham Hartill, writers in residence at HMP & YOI Parc

GH: Hi Billy - has anything interesting happened in your work recently as writer in residence at Parc?

WM: I guess what makes working at Parc so good is that every day is interesting and each individual you work with has a powerful and unique story within them. Recently, though, I've been working with a group of IPP [Indeterminate sentence for Public Protection] prisoners to create a play about IPP, highlighting their plight and the psychological pressures they are under. It has been moving to see these guys produce honest, startling work because they believe in their cause ... vocalising what they see as the injustice of their situation. I think creative writing is one of the few outlets for freedom of expression in prison - would you agree?

GH: Absolutely. I guess the prisoners at Parc are relatively lucky in that there's a good art department and a daily music class too. It's great to meet guys who are discovering their creativity in whatever field for the first time in their lives; sometimes it can be people who had minimal input about books and reading when they were young, but there are a good many who do read and have always wanted to have a go at writing themselves. Many want to write about their lives - this can, I'm sure, have a rehabilitative and therapeutic benefit as the men are sometimes using this work to look at themselves. The other side is that they are using it to boast to themselves in the popular tradition of true crime - to say that they have lived extraordinary lives, that they are some kind of hero. The fact is that many have lived extraordinary lives but not in the way they suspect!

I saw the IPP play - I thought it was very accomplished and a very strong statement; a great example of the way facilitators can help produce a potentially important piece from men who have never written before - to help them find a 'voice', which in this case was the play itself. What will happen to the play now?

WM: There has already been another performance at the Sherman Theatre in Cardiff and we have two further performances planned, including one in London. The play at present runs for twenty minutes but we are developing a full-length stage play.

The performances are outside the prison environment, which for me is important. I think the creative arts can be used to bring the prison population and outside society together. I think they can bring a greater understanding, demystify popular perception of the type of person who ends up inside, and can make a prisoner feel just a little bit as though he or she can have a voice in ordinary society.

I know you have worked with prisoners who have been published as writers, in literary publications not as prisoners per se, but do you think the arts can be a path back into legitimate society for a prisoner?

GH: Well, one would hope so, although of course this would be difficult if not impossible to prove. Writing as an activity,

or intervention, is of course only one aspect of any prisoner's activities inside. One big difference it makes is that it can enable offenders to reflect on themselves, to engage with their own life stories and experiences in a way they may never have done before, as well as being a means to boost self-esteem through discovering creativity. Creative writing can radically change self-perception and alter habitual ways of looking at things and living one's life. How this finds a foothold amidst all the pressures of life on release is of course another matter; it would be great if there were courses available on the outside especially for prisoners who have engaged in the arts and want to continue to do so on release. The Koestler Mentoring Scheme is a certainly step in the right direction.

I completely agree with you when you say that one important thing about prisoners' writing is that only they can tell their stories. The prison walls, it seems to me, are not just a means to keep offenders away from society, but to keep society away from offenders, and the realities of ways of life that lead people into jail. When I started to work in prisons the biggest

The Visit

My aunt came too.

It was only when they'd sidled into their seats that I remembered
what I'd meant to say to mum and dad the night before: 'Please
don't let Pam sit in the middle!'

My worries that she would use the opportunity to persuade me to
'turn to Jesus' were unfounded.

The light above us was flickering. Just enough to stir a little
nausea.

Typical Dad. Instead of accepting 'anything' as an order for
chocolate, he borrowed a selection for me to choose.
Like it was important.

He only cried on the way out this time.

shock to me was not prison life as such but my own heightened perception of the social reality of huge swathes of our population in modern Britain.

WM: There is definitely no hiding when working in prison from the reality of the catastrophic lives many prisoners have lived, and there is also no denying that although each individual's story is unique, there is a commonality to their experiences. One of the privileges of working as a writer in prison is the opportunity to work closely with these men and to be able to build trust in the relationship. It means we can, in some cases, strive to get closer to an emotional truth in the prisoner's work, which must inevitably filter into other areas of their lives. I think it is also beneficial to the prisoner to be working as a collaborator, in many ways an equal partner, as opposed to a student on a course or in a class, or even on a rehabilitation course where a lot of writing is being done.

This can create a dilemma, though, where the emotions that can emerge during writing can have a powerful effect on the prisoner. As you pointed out, they may be finding new ways to look at themselves and the world through writing, but we as writers are not equipped to deal in-depth with the psychological results. There is also the personal responsibility you sometimes feel for someone's well-being that can take a toll on yourself.

In the case of the IPP drama there is a clear objective for the guys involved to get a higher public profile to their feelings of injustice over their sentence, but with an individual the objectives can be far more complex.

GH: I think it's worth concluding by saying how important the Koestler and other awards can be to writers in jail – they really pull their fingers out – especially in finishing and polishing work when Koestler time comes around! They talk about the prize money of course but it's as much about the recognition, and the satisfaction of looking over a piece with pride.

Since 2008 the Koestler Trust has held its annual exhibition at London's Southbank Centre; before that it was held at a variety of London venues, from St Martin-in-the-Fields to the ICA. Below is a list of those who have opened the exhibitions over past years.

2011
Michael Spurr, Chief Executive, National Offender Management Service
John Thornhill, Chair, Magistrates' Association

2010
Crispin Blunt, Prisons Minister
Sarah Philps, Chair, Victim Support

2009
Claire Ward, Under-Secretary of State for Justice

2008
Frances Done, Chair, Youth Justice Board

2007
Grayson Perry, artist
Ekow Eshun, Artistic Director of the ICA

2006
Erwin James, ex-prisoner journalist
Sir Joseph Pilling, former Director General of the Prison Service

2005
Baroness Scotland, Minister for Criminal Justice
Rachel Billington, writer

2004
Benjamin Zephaniah, poet
Luke Sergeant, Governor, HM Prison Wormwood Scrubs

2003
Will Self, writer
Anne Owers, HM Chief Inspector of Prisons

2002
Maggi Hambling, artist

2001
Roger Graef, film maker
Martin Narey, Director General of the Prison Service

2000
Brian Eno, musician
Stephen Shaw, Prisons Ombudsman

1999
Paul Boateng, Minister for Prisons & Probation

1998
Stephen Fry, actor and broadcaster
Jack Straw, Home Secretary

1997
Jeremy Paxman, broadcaster
Joyce Quinn, Minister for Prisons

1996
Princess Anne
Ann Widdecombe, MP
Richard Tilt, Director General of the Prison Service

1995
Brian Eno, musician

1994
Jon Snow, Channel 4 News
Christopher Whitehead, Prison Ombudsman

1993
Judge Stephen Tumim
Peter Cameron, artist

1992
John Mortimer QC, writer

1991
Kenneth Baker, Home Secretary

1990
Judge Stephen Tumim

1989
Princess Anne

1988
Dr John Rae
Lord Ferrers

1987
Baroness Ewart-Briggs

1986
Rabbi Julia Neuberger

1985
Terry Waite

1984
Leon Brittain

1983
Lady Howe

1982
Lord Whitelaw

1981
Michael Foot

1969-80
Sir Huw Weldon
Joyce Grenfell
Ludovic Kennedy
Lord Gardiner
JB Priestley
Lord Home

Acknowledgements

In compiling this book we would like
to thank all the contributors who have
made it what it is - every one of them
has responded with enthusiasm and
generosity, and we are truly grateful.

Many thanks to Michael Scammell and
Faber for kindly allowing us to reprint
the extract from his biography of Arthur
Koestler on pp.6.

Above all, thanks to the many creative
individuals who have submitted work to
the Koestler Trust over the years, and
helped to make it the success it is; without
their inspired and inspiring contributions
we would have little to celebrate.